For all children who are colourblind.

T.P.

Text and illustration copyright © Tom Powell 2021

The rights of Tom Powell to be identified as the author has been asserted by him in accordance with the Copyright Designs and Patents Act 1988.

All rights reserved. No part of this publication may be reproduced, stored in or introduced into a retrieval system or transmitted, in any form, or by any means (electronic, mechanical, photocopying, recording or otherwise) without the prior written permission of the author. Any person who does any unauthorised act in relation to this publication may be liable to criminal prosecution and civil claims for damages.,

The colourblind kid

Tom Powell

For more poems and short stories
visit: authortompowell.com

Young Tim had his coat,
And a bag that was blue.

He had short golden hair,
In spikes stuck with glue.

How Tim did smile,
As he looked at his dad.

Looking to start his day,
Life was not so bad.

For today was special,
Tim's first day of school.
Dressed in his uniform,
He did look cool.

They walked on their way,
Passed the field of green.
Down the small lane,
Up to the gate with
a silver sheen.

Tim waved goodbye to his dad,
And to school he did skip.
Off on his new adventure,
As if in a rocket ship.

Miss Taylor his new teacher,
Purple scarf she did wear.

She had bright green eyes,
And black plaited hair.

"Hello, Tim," she did greet,
"Ready? What do you say?"

"Sit on the blue chair,
"Get ready for your day?"

Young Tim did sit,
But on the blue he did not go.
He sat on the purple,
And went with the flow.

"That's not right!"
Came a voice from behind
"The blue is one more,
Did you lose your mind?"

Next came art,
Tim's favourite by far.
"What should I draw?

A beautiful flower...

"...or a red racing car?"

A picture of his home,
He decided to make.

A gift for his mum,
Fit with sky, dog and lake.

"That's not right!"
A call from the side.

Your lake is purple,
But I can see you tried.

Tim was embarrassed,
For what he had done.

He stopped his drawing,
And decided colour was no fun.

But once again,
A challenge to be had.
"Can I have the green, please?"
Asked a friendly lad.

Tim turned away,
Tears in his eyes.
For he was not sure,
As his tears turned to cries.

Tim did sigh.
"I can't find blue, red or green,
Don't ask me, why?"

Miss Taylor did come,
After hearing Tim's cry.
"Are you colourblind, Tim?
I don't mean to pry."

Tim looked up at her,
as he cleared his voice.
"I mix up my colours,
I'm sorry, it's not my choice."

"No need to say sorry,
For what you can see.
Your colours are yours,
And perfect for me."

"Let's sit down,
And talk with the class.
You can help me explain,
What it's like to see brown grass."

"The way Tim sees,
Might be different from you.
He can see colours,
In a subtle hue."

"Colours are still there,
It's not just black and white.
But they're harder to see,
And not quite as bright."

"Many people are colourblind,
Some with blue, red, or green.
This makes it harder,
For these colours to be seen."

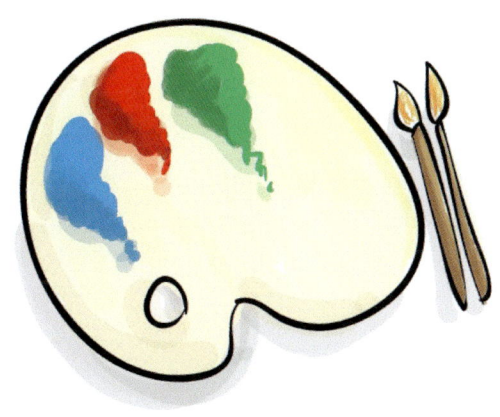

Tim looked up,
A smile on his face.
He wasn't so different,
He wasn't out of place.

Miss Taylor lent forward,
With a secret to tell.
"I thought green,
Was the colour of this shell."

Questions about being colourblind

Are many people colourblind?

Around 1 in 12 men and 1 in 200 women are colourblind. This means that someone is probably colourblind in your class.

Around 5% of people are colourblind.

What does it mean to be colourblind?

It means that they find it difficult to identify and compare between certain colours. The most common is known as red-green colour vision deficiency. In very rare cases, some people can have total colour blindness.

How do you become colourblind?

Colour blindness is usually passed on from parents at birth (inherited), even if the parent isn't colourblind themselves. Sometimes it can develop later on in life.

Why are people colourblind?

People are colourblind because some of the colour-sensitive cells in the eyes, called cones, are either missing or do not work properly.

How do I know if I'm colourblind?

You can ask for a test from your optician. There are also tests you can do online to see if you are colourblind. In these tests you will have to pick objects in different colours or order colours in shades.

Printed in Great Britain
by Amazon